From Famine to Feast

From Famine to Feast:
My Thoughts About My Eating Disorder.

K. Michelle Pahl

eBook ISBN 978-1-7776115-1-4
Paperback ISBN 978-1-7776115-0-7

Editor: K. Michelle Pahl
Cover Art by conger design (Pixaby).

Thank you.

I'd love a list of the people I'm supposed to acknowledge and thank. Accuracy is essential: omission guilt will gnaw at me for decades.

Also, what kind of thanks am I offering? Should I be formal, or should I gush? Should I be giving Hallmark movie-level thanks? [1]

Do I alphabetize to avoid the appearance of favouritism?

Can I make a chart?

How far back should I go? I've fond memories of my grade seven teacher, but referencing Mr. Doerksen might be overkill for all that I loved *Treasure Island*. Plus, if I mention him, I have to give a shout-out to Miss Breeden, my grade one teacher: what if it never stops?

The great thing about anxiety is its eagerness to make things more complicated.

Should I thank the staff and patients from my most recent residential treatment? [2] I'm grateful they helped me choose life.

A "hello" as well to the ones who didn't make it. I miss you. I hope you're resting easy.

To proceed then, while noting that errors and omissions are an accident of memory: no hurt is intended.

Thank you to my parents, especially my mother, who fought hard to keep me alive. I don't say it often, but I appreciate everything you've done. I'd have chosen a perfect daughter for you if I'd been given the option.

Thank you to the friends who fought for me as well. I appreciate your help even while worrying about battle fatigue. Thank you for the talks, the hugs, and the laughter. Thank you for the music, the dancing, and the general merriment.

Thank you to my psychiatrist, Dr. Strauss, who's not only part of the "keep Michelle alive" team but suggested this compilation book.

Thank you to my therapist, Cecilia Mannella, MSW, BSW. I wouldn't be here without her.

Thank you to the people who read my blog. I'm grateful for your interest and support. It makes me happy in my bones. Thanks especially to the people who comment and engage.

Finally, thank you to my children. We all need a reason to keep fighting. You're mine. Even if I don't always make that clear.

Table of Contents

Introduction: Thoughts About Writing A Book.

I'm putting together a collection of my twelve most popular blog posts!

I'm so excited! I'm going to have an official, albeit self-published, albeit mostly e-version, book.

I'm putting together a collection of my twelve most popular blog posts.

I'm kind of excited. I think. Maybe. It might not be very good.

I'm putting together a collection of my twelve most popular blog posts. This was a mistake. Writing a book was a terrible idea.

What was I thinking? What was my doctor thinking? I'm a hack with no experience beyond blogging to a relatively small audience. A book by someone like me seems arrogant and over-the-top.

(I can hear my therapist saying, *"Why not you?"* as I type. Unfortunately, other voices are busy too: *"Who do you think you are?"* they want to know. I can feel depression's laughter and my eating disorder's scorn over the very idea.)

I should know by now not to agree to things I haven't fully considered.

I'm going to get, *"let me think about it, and I'll get back to you,"* tattooed on my everywhere.

Publishing a "best of the blog" was my psychiatrist's idea. It smells like personal growth with a side of "let's keep her busy now that she's not taking the mood stabilizer." [3] It has "potential for disaster" writ large. There are so many ways to spin this into proof of my failure as a human being.

But a promise is a promise, and I try to avoid being a coward.

That last bit sounds good, doesn't it? In truth, I've no idea if I'm a particular coward or not: I suspect I might be. Who can tell: situations that require extreme bravery aren't always thick on the ground. Although repeatedly fighting the same battle is brave, or so various memes on social media assure us.

Step one, "writing" the book, was easy. It's a compilation of my twelve most popular blog posts: it's practically written already. [4]

The great thing about having my blog on Word Press is they do the heavy lifting. They collect the statistics I tend to ignore for fear they'll distress.[5] I don't need to know how many people aren't reading me at any given moment. That data, however, remains available despite my determined denial. Generating a top twelve list is simply a matter of applying the right filter.

Step two is perfecting the posts while updating the blog with any changes I make. [6] I've been repeating the mantra, "good enough is good enough," to give myself permission to be done. Perfectionism is just a way to avoid publishing and risking rejection.

Step three is formatting. The book's appearance is one of the things I'm using as an excuse to avoid publishing. That's either ironic or an amusing coincidence. An eating disorder is, after all, in part about perfecting the appearance.

What are the issues? I don't like the font choices, the table of contents has too many capital letters, and I can't sprinkle images here, there, and everywhere.

Being cute and clever is also frowned upon.

The font problem is out of my control – the only options for Kindle publishing are serif or sans – and fixing the table of contents, while possible, would mean new titles. I struggled to come up with the existing ones the first time. Titles are not my strength.

I tell myself to let it go. There are worse things than slightly-imperfect aesthetics.

Said the "go team" voice of the woman struggling with eating disorder recovery.

Letting go is easier said than done. Aesthetics are important to me (depression-based lack of personal attention notwithstanding). Straight lines, balance, and symmetry are beautiful. Precision hath charms that soothe the anxious breast. [7]

I'm not currently purging (almost a year and a half now), but the voice demanding perfection is persistent. If I'm not perfecting myself, then perfect everything else. It can make folding and putting away clothes a challenge: it can make accepting *Times New Roman* as the *de facto* font choice impossible. How can I be worth anything as a human being if my T-shirts aren't tight envelopes and I can't use a trendy, over-exposed font? [8]

Requiring perfection prevents forward movement. Nothing is good enough, so you stay where you are until it is. That day never comes: there's no growth because you are, still, imperfect. It's not really about beauty. It's about control and risk. About clutching the former and avoiding the latter.

I'm surprised perfectionism lets me publish in a consistent-ish fashion. My writing is nowhere close to pristine, occasional delusional-daydreams, notwithstanding.

I'm amazed and grateful people both read and liked my early efforts. I feel I owe them an apology.

In the early days, I thought refusing to use capital letters and eschewing proofreading made me authentic. It turns out I was sloppy and arrogant. "Sloppy" might seem a strange choice considering my eating disorder's perfectionist bent, but arrogance is a true story. Misplaced, as it turns out.

I thought the lower case would make me the next e. e. cummings. I was mistaken. 9

Step four is collective: it's the last bits and pieces that have to be taken care of before "P" day. It's proofreading one last time, adding the ISBN to the manuscript, and dealing with the inside voice that says abandon this and head for the hills.

It's odd when one of your secret dreams approaches fruition. I'm going to crank the stereo and dance like a madwoman when the book goes live before ordering a hard copy of my very own.

You wake up every morning to fight
the same demons that left you so tired
the night before, and that, my love,
is bravery.

One: My Eating Disorder Rules, of Which There Are Many.

The list is chronological, and the oldest rules are the easiest to remember: they've had the most time to bake. The rules overlap in their requirements at times; one rule leads to the next, and so on.

I don't have to worry about what they are. The rules are just there, built into my bones, ever-present, directing the eating, restricting, binging, purging, and other eating disorder-related behaviours.

The following isn't a complete list. The production of it was more triggering than I imagined it would be, as is realizing I still adhere to many of them. It's eye-opening to see how many resemble the rules in the monthly, lose-ten-pounds-by-the-weekend diet articles that are forever published.

We take in more than we think. It's less benign than we hope.

The rules are inflexible and keep me focused on my eating disorder. They're designed to keep me trapped. It's hard to have independent thoughts that do not, in some way, circle back to my ED. That bitch follows me everywhere. She is determined and persistent.

1. Everything gets measured.

I don't follow this one much anymore in terms of restricting, but I sometimes measure to ensure I'm getting enough food. I tend to under-estimate. In the early days of my eating disorder, I measured everything. You get familiar with how quantities appear. Breakfast for years was a third of a cup of bran buds and a third of a cup of milk – until I switched out the milk for water. Even after I altered my behaviour from primarily restricting to primarily purging, I still monitored my non-binge eating intake compulsively.

2. Special plates and utensils.

A one-third cup portion looks pathetic on a regular, grownup-sized plate: it looks fine, however, if you use dessert bowls and salad plates. Using smaller utensils such as teaspoons and salad forks was also a rule.

Once I was on my own, the serving plates changed again. I used either a small mixing bowl – for salad or steamed veggies – or an odd, plastic toy plate. You know you value yourself when you make yourself eat from a child's toy.

3. No butter.

Butter was one of the first foods to go. First, I eliminated added butter; later, it was anything that had butter as an ingredient. This inevitably evolved into:

4. No added fat.

When I gave up butter, I still allowed myself a scraping of mayo or a drizzle of salad dressing. Those 'indulgences' were the next to go. Why use mayonnaise when mustard has no calories or fat? Why use salad dressing when vinegar, salt, and powdered garlic make a tasty dressing? So very delicious. Or not, but that's the lie you tell yourself. You're too fat for added anything and not deserving of tasty anyway.

5. On the side.

My eating disorder is a fan of deconstruction. I have no interest in how the chef wants the dish prepared and presented. Sauce goes on the side, and "extras" are separated from the main. We don't need wasted calories. Why would you put sauce on your pasta when briefly dipping your fork's tines in the adjacent dish before twirling up the noodles provides practically the same experience? On the bright side, I only dealt with sauce on the side for a bit.

6. No pasta.

The end game for the eating disorder is no food at all. You think I'd have made that connection early on, but despite living through periods where the only things "allowed" were iceberg lettuce and steamed carrots, I did not.

Pasta was eliminated later in the game than some foods, but it had preconditions attached to consumption before it was finally retired. It had to be plain. The style was irrelevant: they could be fettucine or spirals or macaroni. No stuffed noodles or layered pasta dishes were allowed.

I ate it with a "dressing" made of low-calorie fake butter and salt, and if I ate it, there was nothing else until the next day. That could be challenging if noodles were your lunchtime meal.

There's a reason why gum is popular with the eating disorder set. It takes the place of food.

7. No meat.

Meat was eliminated early on. It was the first complete food group I rejected. I told my family I was embracing vegetarianism, but it was just an excuse to eat low-calorie foods. Meat was simply too caloric to consume. Plus, if you reject meat, you can also reject sauces and stews and dishes that contain it, further reducing consumption.

8. Only eat the outside of foods. Only eat the edges.

I started with bread. I love bread, but it got less thrilling without butter – at least until I discovered low-cal fake butter sprinkles. They're not great on the flesh, but they're kind of tasty on the crust. Eating only the crust meant fewer calories: that was always a good thing.

Edge-crust eating is furtive. It's eating without eating, even though you make a note of it in your daily tally. Just a bite to silence hunger pangs is all you need. The stomach can be so pathetically grateful.

You pick the crunchy bits from the edge of a casserole while getting water from the fridge and wonder, how many calories in a noodle? You pinch a tiny corner from an entrée, a crumb of a cookie from the bottom of the bag. It's eating but not. You're hungry, but you're "dieting," so a crumb is as much of an indulgence as you can allow. Your body can't be trusted anyway.

9. Nothing fried.

Fried foods are an absolute no. They're the road to instant fat. I was definitely not allowed to eat anything that came from a vat. No french fries, no chicken burgers, no fried fish, no nachos – no chips of any kind, no to a hundred very tasty things because one bite would obviously lead to my body doubling in size. And it was already too fat. Which meant I was worthless.

10. Even numbers.

My need for even numbers applies across a variety of situations. Food is not an exception.

The number of pieces I cut something into. The number of pieces I eat. The number of units I buy (it's hard to count tiny things without drawing attention to yourself). The number of reps I perform when exercising. Goal numbers may change over time, but my preference for even numbers remains the same.

Laxatives must be taken in even numbers. Binge foods must be eaten in even numbers: ten cookies or twelve, but never eleven. Everything that happens should be divisible by two. I have no idea where the rule came from, but it's existed as far back as I can remember.

11. No dairy.

Once I gave up meat, the next big calorie cut came from eliminating dairy. No cheese – too fattening. No milk, because you're giving up cereal. No yogurt, unless it's the zero fat, zero sugar, zero texture, and zero flavour diet version. Eaten with a tiny spoon, of course.

12. No liquid calories.

Alcohol is excluded from the "no liquid calories" rule as long as I get rid of an equal or better number of food calories in compensation. I usually add extra exercise as well, just in case. No other liquids with calories are acceptable. No soup, no milk, no juice, no smoothies, no shakes. Nothing but water and diet pop. Diet pop is your friend and companion. Who needs food when there's diet cola?

13. Calories matter.

The content of what I was eating was less important than the calorie count. I gave up meat, but I didn't replace the protein. I just considered it a win in the restriction column. I gave up dairy but didn't replace the calcium. I gave up complex carbs but didn't replace the fibre.

Eating disorders are a symphony of loss, and they're unconcerned with nutrition or long-term health. I often ate my allowed six-hundred calories in the form of two chocolate bars. I couldn't eat them as a snack: snacks don't exceed fifty calories. It's best if you can eliminate snacks altogether.

14. No homemade food, especially baked goods.

You can't know what's in them, so you can't accurately calculate the calorie count. Homemade items from other people are *verboten* always. I'm not sure what I imagine, someone hiding in their kitchen, magically adding calories to their cookies before serving them, I suppose.

15. No food after six o'clock.

Period. Hunger is irrelevant. You don't eat after dinner. If you do, it's a binge, and you'd best be throwing that stuff up.

16. Never take the elevator.

My eating disorder regularly reminded me that lazy people take the elevator or escalator. If you want to be thin, you walk. Never mind that you're carrying a new microwave and your apartment is on the thirteenth floor. You're walking.

These sixteen rules are part of what felt like an infinite number. I was often overwhelmed and exhausted by the expectations. There were a lot of demands to meet, and failure to adhere was not an option. Justifications or time off weren't allowed.

The ostensible goal is perfection. The secret plan is death. The misery the ED brings on the road to the grave is just a side benefit. [10]

(February 22, 2018)

Two: I'm More Than Just My Body.

I'm more than just my body.

This is my affirmation for today. Similar positive statements I've used have included:

I don't have to be thin; I'm more than my appearance; I'm allowed to take up space, and *I'm more than numbers on a scale.*

Affirmations are easy to say, hard to believe, and nearly impossible for me to live. Buy-in is challenging when you have decades of accepting the opposite.

I'm more than just my body. Why is it so easy to believe my internal critic's contentions to the contrary?

I'm kind. I'm accepting. I'm a good friend and mother. I'm reasonably intelligent and have a sufficient number of accomplishments. Unfortunately, these truths and others are rendered irrelevant if my pants feel too tight or the reflection in the mirror doesn't display obvious bones.

Well-meaning friends and family offer encouragements. Affirmations to-go. They list my accomplishments and throw compliments my way. It doesn't help all that much. It's kind and flattering, but I don't believe a word they say. It's hard to stand against the inside voice, which is convincingly familiar about the opposite. It's hard to believe good things.

They don't feel like mine, the compliments. I don't feel them in my bones. I don't believe them in my guts. The kind words are washed away by my belief that nothing I do has value or worth if my body is imperfect. Perfect being skeletal to a level I've yet to achieve: no matter the number, the eating disorder's response is "not yet." Perhaps dead and decomposing?

I'm more than my body. I'm more than my bones. I'm more than a meat suit stumbling haphazardly through life. I have value beyond my outline, and I will repeat my affirmations *ad nauseum* until the reflection in the mirror doesn't lead to double-checking my measurements. Until I believe the affirmations I struggle to say and am no longer consumed with self-criticism.

Until I really am more than just my body.

(February 2, 2018)

Three: Failing at My Eating Disorder.

I'm failing at my eating disorder, and my eating disorder reminds me of that fact incessantly. She's a bitch that way.

I feel bad about failing, which is odd, considering it's mourning the absence of destructive behaviours. We miss what we know, even when it's harmful: we miss the loss of the familiar.

I'm failing because I'm eating. That's a huge failure when you have an eating disorder. The goal of my eating disorder, consumption-wise, is zero. It regularly reminds me to eat less. "Less is more" because the eating disorder is in it to win it, even if "winning" means starving to death.

I'm failing because I'm not purging. I'm failing less often with binging: I still struggle there. It's mostly on food I've not been allowed to consume without repercussions (vomiting). I suspect the bingeing is a big, angry, "fuck you" at the years of restrictions and purges. That I've not purged in response to these lapses in control and ingestion of extra calories is irritating my eating disorder no end: unfortunately, when she's irked, her language can be unkind.

Fat. Pathetic. Failure.

She's not happy with the way my pants fit today. It's a chink in my armour.

Part of the problem is the gap between what I thought recovery would be and what it is. More specifically, the gap between what I thought I'd look like in recovery and my reality.

In my mind, in recovery, I look thin. Very thin, eating disorder thin. In my mind, in recovery, I eat normally, indulge occasionally, and keep baked goods in the house, all with a perfect body.

That's not recovery. That's letting my eating disorder dictate the terms of its *faux* surrender – a bizarre proposal, to be sure.

Calling successes "failures" is also not recovery. That's letting the eating disorder control the narrative.

Unfortunately, I'm a little conflicted about letting it wholly go. I want to be free. I'm tired of my eating disorder, more tired than I can explain. I want my brain back. I want to stop connecting my sense of self-worth to the size of my jeans. I want to stop wasting time on irrelevant and pointless trains of thought. I feel petty and shallow in my disorder. I'm sad I've given such time and space to something that's ultimately irrelevant, though writing my eating disorder off as only-vanity minimizes its helpfulness in my survival.

You find examples of people's weird and untenable behaviours everywhere, and they all have one thing in common – they're designed to help the architects carry on. We do what we need to do to survive, and sometimes, that manifests in strange and harmful. Our choices may not serve us well, but they do save us. For a time. In the end, we have to let maladaptive coping tricks go before they destroy us.

But I digress.

I know I need the eating disorder gone. I know I need to keep failing. I get it: eating disorders kill. Even so, a small piece of my brain is asking if it was all really that bad. Can't we just peacefully co-exist? So that we can be thin. Just until we're perfect.

You have to admire the eating disorder's tenacity.

Her will to live is why letting my eating disorder decide what recovery should look like is a bad idea. But it's hard to pull free from her tentacles; it's hard to identify who's speaking at times, me or bulimia. We've lived together so long: we're enmeshed and entwined.

My eating disorder tells me I'm failing at recovery, but among the myriad of things I don't know, there are some things I do. I know the disease doesn't dictate the cure. I know recovery isn't deciding today will be horrible because the waistband of your pants feels tight, and you should cut back on what you eat, and why aren't you on the elliptical already?

I know that recovery is being willing to let the harmful things go. Sometimes, I even am. And that's winning, regardless of what my eating disorder tries to say.

(January 22, 2019)

Four: A Lot Like Me.

I stood behind a woman at the checkout counter at the pet store this morning: she was very thin – I'm pretty sure she has an eating disorder.

It's not just that the thin was extreme and borderline-hospitalization level. I've encountered plenty of thin people who don't have eating disorders. I wonder about them.

How do they stay thin without obsessive thoughts and self-hatred? How do they exercise without going over the top? Are they okay with people noticing them, with the attention their small bodies garner? Maybe they don't constantly compare themselves to others, although my brain can barely take that on board. Constant comparison is a common eating disorder behaviour (it's becoming more common in the "normal" world too).

She didn't look healthy. She wasn't thin in a way that made you feel good. She was skinny in a way that made you think of campaigns that raise money for malnourished children overseas.

She was wearing the heavily blinged-out pants favoured by the teen set. You can wear what you like, but it seemed incongruous considering her age and attempts at invisibility. They were enormous, engulfing her diminutive frame. I wonder if they used to fit or were bought in size far-too-large, another common eating disorder thing.

The pants seemed empty as well as sparkly. They sagged from the belt into empty-looking legs that seemed to balance on thick-soled, skateboarder-style sneakers, thanks only to the strength of the denim. However, the hands that poked out from the oversized hoodie confirmed the existence of limbs.

It was her face that made me think of anorexia as the explanation. I caught a glimpse of her profile when she turned towards the cashier. People with eating disorders have a look to the lower face and jaw: it's something in the musculature, in the set to the face, the cast of the mouth. I see it. I've wondered before if the non-afflicted do. Maybe it's a case of "like speaks to like."

Her hair reminded me of a friend of mine. I met Lily years ago when we spent time as eating disorder in-patients together. She had what I've come to recognize as eating disorder hair: oddly wig-like and too much for the head; a perceptual reaction to the thinness of the face, perhaps. The hair is not one's crowning glory when you starve yourself and eliminate all fat. Lily's hair was always dry and brittle; this woman's hair looked much the same. She sported the same "I don't care about myself as a human being" ugly ponytail I often wear.

I wonder what I looked like to other people when my eating disorder was at its worst? I wonder if I looked that unhappy and frail when I was out and about?

Her eyes caught my attention before she looked back at the floor. They looked tired, with bags that made her overly-pale skin look bruised. Skip foods with iron long enough, and you, too, can be whiter than white. The worst thing about the eyes was the familiarity of the expression within. The despair. The defeat. The look you have when you give up because the fight's too hard, and you can't do it anymore, and what difference does it make anyhow?

The clothes were familiar too. She could have raided my closet to get dressed. This is not fashion-forward dressing. This is how you dress when you're hiding. Because you think you're too gross for anything else, you wear what will hide your body. Even when you get thin. Because you're not quite thin enough. One day. Soon.

The camouflage is important for audiences foreign and domestic. If you can't see my body, you won't see it's lacking. You won't notice it, and therefore my, essential wrongness. If I can't see my body, then perhaps I won't notice how gross and fat and wrong I am either. Maybe then the inside voice will take some time off.

Kidding. She never takes time off.

After a while, I started to pretend the incredibly oversized look was stylish. I pretended I dressed the way I did because I was an original. That wearing jeans four sizes too big and giant men's t-shirts was fashionable. That my efforts to hide my body were a personal choice unconnected to my eating disorder. That I didn't have a problem.

Her body language reinforced the clothing's vibe. Her head stayed down most of the time, tucked into her chest between hunched shoulders as she avoided eye contact with the cashier during the transaction. She kept her body mostly angled away from the cashier and me, cutting off access and exposure. Her arms wrapped her torso, and she only half-unwound when it was time to pay. She left quickly too, and quietly, with her head still down. Her walk to the door was almost a run and so damn familiar. Everything about her presence screamed, "don't look at me." Everything about her exit screamed "escape."

I used to walk quickly all the time. I used to think I liked walking that way; that warp speed was my speed. It was easier to fool myself when I lived in the city. Everyone walks quickly. It was easy to pretend the racing wasn't avoiding people. It wasn't me trying to flee.

Part of me wanted to be intrusive and talk to her. I wanted to know if I was right. I wanted to see if she was all right. I wanted to help.

I made no moves as I watched her walk out the door. Because although I wanted to help, I was also glad to see her go. Eating disorder memories are not where I like to spend my time.

And then there's the jealousy. That used to be me. My eating disorder is rubbing her hands, thrilled to encounter such an extreme example of thin for comparison purposes. She knows her audience: I was curious and concerned, but I also lusted after the emaciated accomplishment. Sometimes, recovery feels like failure. What good am I if I'm not damaged?

Berating yourself for no longer abusing yourself is a touch ironic.

It's hard, though, to let the defective wiring go.

(February 5, 2018)

Five: An Eating Disorder Journal Entry.

From my journal this week, thoughts about the struggle that is recovery:

"I binged and purged last night. It was the fat thoughts that got me. I've gained about ten pounds, and the weight that is supposed to help me is killing me, or at least that's what it feels like.

Thinner, thinner, thinner is all I think about now. Diet hard, exercise harder. Forget quitting smoking; forget friends and family. Forget writing, forget recovery, forget life. Forget everything but getting thin, back to bones.

All I feel is the flesh of my middle. My legs feel enormous – fat and cellulite-ridden. Imperfect and unworthy.

Everything in my life seems pointless. Nothing is any good if I can't be thin.

I'm trying to argue, to rationalize, to logic and talk my way out. I'm trying something new. Exercise, but to make myself strong and healthy. Keep on eating. Visualize Jennifer Lopez's body – she's not a stick, and she's the same age as me. Want that.

It's not working.

I want sticks. I want bones.

The eating disorder thoughts make my anxiety worse, which is ironic since anxiety drives the eating disorder in the first place. Increased depression comes next, and then feelings of worthlessness, which lead back to not liking myself much and calling myself "fat," so it's off to the mirror again to tell myself, "I love you," notwithstanding my purchase of low-calorie meal replacement bars to consume in lieu of food, which probably comes under the category of "situational irony."

(May 12, 2019)

Five B: Saying, "I Love You" to Myself.

I recently reread Cheryl Richardson's *"The Art of Extreme Selfcare."* I bought it a couple of years ago and read it cover to cover at the time. I took notes, highlighted essential passages, and implemented nothing. Change, even positive change, is challenging and can be difficult to implement. We cling to our default settings with our dying grasp, even when they're harmful.

I've been dissatisfied with my life of late. I'm frustrated and so went looking for something to give me a kick-start change. I scanned the self-help titles that litter my bookshelves for inspiration, and Ms. Richardson's jumped out. Probably because it's slightly oversized.

I grabbed it and planned to reread, thinking that maybe this time, I'd adopt some of the recommendations.

One of the first topics is self-acceptance and self-love. That was less than thrilling: I'd hoped to start with manageable. "Make the bed" or something like that. Ms. Richardson points out that a lack of self-love is something we need to fix sooner rather than later. She suggests a simple exercise: pause and say, "I love you, *blank*" to your reflection every time you catch sight of it. [11] In the morning, when you're brushing your teeth. Every time you pass by a mirror. You might want to do that last one in your head if you're at the mall.

It's a good suggestion that made me cringe. Loving myself is not my default setting. I'm more comfortable with ugly language. Words like *ugly, stupid, moronic, pathetic, and fat* are soothingly familiar.

I decided to go ahead despite my resistance. Leaning into the discomfort will make my therapists proud. What's the worst that could happen? Perhaps not the best attitude to hold while approaching change, but whatever. After all, beyond making me feel foolish, how hard could it be?

As it turns out, saying "I love you" to myself is difficult indeed.

The procedure is this: I face the mirror, look myself in the eye (did you know you can't look at yourself in both eyes), and say the words. *I love you.* I feel ridiculous and very much the liar.

The mirror makes it particularly hard. It occurred to me as I stood there, absorbing my uncomfortable response, that notwithstanding the work I've done in recovery, I still don't look at myself very much. I don't like what I see. I glance, but only long enough to check for facial imperfections and added fat. That's still what mirrors are to me; a verification system for my neuroses. Mirrors exist to point out all the ways I'm wrong. I rarely look at myself in a kind, supportive, and loving way.

Doing it felt utterly wrong.

This made me sad and not just for myself: where I go, so do others. Although we're unique, we're not that unique. What's true for me is true for many.

How awful is it that so many of us don't love ourselves? Or even like. We don't give ourselves props, and we don't prop ourselves up. The lucky among us feel warmly tolerant. Affection for the self in the developed world has become a rare trait. That's not good enough.

Why isn't the art of loving ourselves taught along the way? Why isn't there a "Like Yourself" unit every year at school or a children's club merit badge on developing a good view of oneself?

Nevertheless, in the spirit of Elizabeth Warren and despite feeling icky, I persist. 12

I love you, Em.

I love you, Em.

I love you, Em.

I hate it when people are right. It's perverse, I know, but part of me would be okay if the dark, dreary, and negative voices were correct. It's nice to be right, even if it's about the wrong thing.

Ms. Richardson was correct. It does get easier. I feel a little less ridiculous every time I share the love. It's started to make me smile. I feel a slight easing in my chest when I hear myself speak.

It's not universal. I'm not full of love for myself and my body all the time just yet. But there's liking and acceptance on the horizon, and I can say, "I love you" to myself without curling my lip.

And if I don't always mean it, I also don't not mean it. So, I might as well keep doing it. What's the worst that could happen?

(May 8, 2019)

Six: Happy Ever After.

I'm a sucker for a book with a happy ending. I prefer it when things work out the way they're supposed to, and by "supposed to," I mean the main character gets their heart's desire, and any and all problems are tidily resolved. Perfect happiness and a perfect life that lasts forever after the last page is turned.

I know it's not reality: I don't care. I like the way I feel when everything turns out all right for the imaginary people I'm invested in. [13]

I read books all the time, both fiction and non. I enjoy the latter well enough: learning new things is a thrill – pineapples are berries – but when I'm down, I want to escape. I want the warm fuzzies you don't get when reading about generals and war. I don't need real-world endings in my escapism, thank you very much.

And they lived happily ever after, at least until Sabrina found out Steve had lied about his finances. Steve found out Sabrina spent two hours every day on a "maintenance" beauty routine that cost four-hundred dollars every month. That's when the daily bickering started.

The books I read range from one-hour series romances to multi-hour, complicated efforts, but they all have satisfying resolutions in common. I read other fiction but generally prefer my choices over the "should" books that are doing the rounds.

I like romance. I don't even mind if it's the main plotline. Love stories make me happy. The romance genre gets zero respect despite amazingly skilled writers, a function of sexism I'm not getting into right now. Even the mysteries and horror stories I choose have love connections and relationship subplots. I want people and relationship stories, even amidst zombie carnage.

I keep many of the books I read. I like libraries but owning the stories I love feels vital to me; books are not on the list when I Marie Kondo my house. I like to revisit them, some a multiplicity of times. They're old friends. I don't need to reread the whole thing, just the chapters leading to the happy dénouement.

I used to be embarrassed by the number of books I have around the house, but e-books brought the solution. No one knows the little tablet you're toting has hundreds of books stored inside. Technology is terrific, although you don't technically own the e-books. Instead, you have lifetime access until you die or the company becomes insolvent. Fingers crossed for Kindle.

There was a time in my life when the only books I'd read were dark and ugly. Truth or fiction, the books hurt; they were about misery, dysfunction, and pain. I thought they'd be an outlet for the darkness inside but reading them made things worse. As it turns out, counterbalancing with light is a better choice. Wallowing in the pit, even a fictional one, isn't helpful.

When things in my life seem especially dire, I turn to the shelves with the oldest of books – meaning the ones I've had the longest. I have some that are technically older, including an enormous dictionary I bought at a garage sale, but the shelves I focus on when I'm in distress are those that hold the children's books.

From Famine to Feast.

There's no better therapeutic escape than rereading the stories I loved as a child. I have multiple shelves dedicated to kids' books only. Fairy tales mix with fantasies like Susan Cooper's, *The Dark is Rising*. Madeleine L'Engle's *Time Quintet* shares space with L.M Montgomery's *Anne* and Laura Ingalls. All of it makes me happy.

I find rereading meditative. I sink into the words and drift away from the world. I'm in the book, no longer myself, unaware of things around and inside. I've always read this way; the book takes over, and I vanish.

I used to be ashamed of my tastes. They seemed simple, wrong like so many of the things I do. I'd hide the books I loved; I worried people would look down on my choices. That's one advantage of recovery and age. You start to worry less about what other people think. At least, that's the plan.

I like books with a happy ever after. Sue me. There's dark and dire in the world already. I don't need it in my escapes.

(August 19, 2019)

Seven: Confrontation and Motivation.

I hate confrontations in an incredibly, big-time way. I'll do almost anything to avoid them, usually to my detriment. I don't stand up for myself: I don't share my feelings if I've been hurt. I'm determined not to rock the boat.

It's not a policy that works well. For me, at any rate. It works fine for the people I don't challenge. And because I don't call them to account, they never think twice about doing the same thing. Why would they? I've made it clear there are no real consequences for ill-treatment.

It's because I'm afraid. I worry that standing up for myself, or disagreeing even, will lead to my rejection. I sacrifice everything to avoid being alone.

We're social creatures: the threat of ostracism chills us to our marrow, and we do what we can to avoid it. But some of us take it too far, accept too much. We're willing to suffer harm rather than say what we think or draw a boundary. We're willing to bury the pain and pretend we aren't bleeding to avoid a tense scene. We live life afraid. It gets tiring and old.

*

I'm not going to Mexico.

I'm not going to Mexico twice.

The first trip was a destination wedding featuring a week in the sun, which I love, in Cancun, which I love, with a large group of friends, some of whom I'm very fond of indeed.

I paid the deposit. I joined the Facebook group chat. I planned my first drink and song request. I looked for a new bathing suit that didn't make me want to cry. I put a celebration sticker on the calendar on the departure date. It was only then that I realized I wouldn't be finished with my radiation treatments before it was time to depart.

"Devastated" sums it up. And pissed. Cancer is a downer. I vented my upset to a different group of friends who'd come by to cheer me up, and in the middle of the chat, we came to a decision. We'd do Mexico ourselves. We'd book for the beginning of April and have a post-cancer girls' trip.

New posts emerged in the group chat. This trip to Mexico or that one? Dolphins or not? Are we interested in ruins? After a bit, things quieted down, but the occasional suggestion still popped up. Like the deal for a trip to Mazatlán I shared. My phone rang about an hour later. It was Karen.

I'm sorry, she said. *We were looking online, and we found a great deal. We booked it because we need a vacation.*

Half of us were suddenly out of a girls' trip.

So much for my post-radiation party.

I was beyond upset and ended the call. I was honest at least: I'm proud of that. I didn't simply hang up: I told Karen I needed to go. I didn't want to cry in front of someone who'd hurt me. The trip we'd set to coincide with finishing radiation, the vacation we'd planned to make up for the one cancer caused me to miss, was off because people got impatient.

I didn't even know how to process what had happened. To not even tell me. To be so unwilling to wait three weeks.

It was a bad night: I was counting on that trip. I couldn't believe they'd taken away the one thing I looked forward to as I headed to radiation every day.

It's been a difficult few months. My depression has been awful, I'm losing another tooth, my parents have health issues, my home life is complicated, and I have cancer. It's low-grade cancer, but still. And now my reward has been yanked away.

I really wasn't sure what to do about my feelings of betrayal.

What have I done to date? I stood my ground, and I'm pretty proud of that.

I talked to Karen. I told her I was angry and hurt. It was terrifying. I was expecting an attack. I was expecting to be abandoned as a friend forthwith. But I'm tired of being a doormat.

I shared my truth. She prevaricated and tried to make excuses. And then, she apologized.

The apology was nice: it's not how I expect things to go when I stand up for myself. It was good to stare fear down and prove it wrong. Unfortunately, the apology changes nothing. My Mexico trip is cancelled once again.

*

I didn't hear from my other friend, who we'll call Susan, for at least a week. She chose not to contact me until I sent out a group text asking about some glasses found. I got a two-line response saying "no" to the glasses and "I'm sorry" regarding Mexico.

I'll get over the disappointment. I'll forgive, and we'll move on in some fashion. But the friendships have been altered, and my sense of trust damaged, at least temporarily.

*

I realized some things following this depressing debacle.

First, it's good to check in with a neutral party in cases of extreme emotion. Another point is view can be helpful. I'd started to wonder if I was overreacting? If maybe it was my fault in some way? If perhaps I shouldn't be upset because they hadn't intended harm?

Was I allowed to think their behaviour selfish?

The people I checked in with backed me up. Karen and Susan's actions sucked. They cancelled the "post-cancer-treatment girls' trip" and made alternative plans without even talking to me. At no point did they let me know what they'd done. Their protestations after-the-fact, that they meant no harm, that we could do another trip later, felt hollow.

Having your feelings validated is a good thing. It helped me hold my space when Karen called back to talk. It allowed me to express myself more clearly. It made me strong enough to say, *"You know what? I'm angry and sad and hurt, and you can't fix that. I'm allowed to feel these things, and I will feel them until I don't.*

It doesn't mean we aren't friends. It means that I feel bad, and you'll have to wait until I feel better."

Challenge people who hurt you. Speak your truth. You're allowed to feel what you feel. You're allowed to talk about it.

I also realized this:

You can't make external things your reason for living. I put too much weight on the trip, a thing "out there." "Out there" is beyond your control, and things happen. Any number of things could have prevented me from going. [14] The promise of something good in the future can't be the thing that's holding your life together. That's not being in control of your life. You have to live in the now.

Fate doesn't much care what you have planned or how much you want it, anyhow.

(January 21, 2020)

Eight: The Annoying Endurance of Chronic Pain.

I suffer from chronic pain. My version is neuralgia. Neuralgia is a "stabbing, burning, and often severe pain due to an irritated or damaged nerve." The nerves can be anywhere in the body. Mine are in my head. I have troublesome left and right trigeminal nerves due to damage I sustained in a car accident twenty-three years ago.

I should've held out for a bigger insurance settlement.

Neuralgia is agonizing. I struggle to find words that will explain its full awfulness. *Misery. Agony. Torture.*

It's like having a pickaxe slam into my head at random intervals twenty-four hours a day for close to a week, ten to twelve times a year. The pain is crazy-making.

I function when it flares. I take my pills. I get up. I go out. I do things. I write. I don't exercise much, but I do carry on with life (albeit with a degree of bitching and moaning). But because I carry on, because I'm not prostrate and screaming, people start to think it's not that bad.

And when I can't pull it together, when I can't rise above the pain to think much less function and beg off visits and plans, they get testy. There's a downside to soldiering on. People fail to appreciate that there's a struggle.

But what am I supposed to do? Take to my bed for a week every month or three weeks? Because that's how often I get attacks. Ten to fifteen times a year, seven days at a time, for twenty-three years. Should I give up that much of my life to prove I suffer? What good would that do? How, exactly, would hiding out serve me?

Neuralgia is one of the leading causes of suicide among chronic pain sufferers. This doesn't surprise. It's utterly brutal.

There's surgical treatment available. You can have the problematic nerves severed. It's not risk-free: possible side effects include trouble swallowing, trouble breathing, and facial paralysis. I haven't signed up.

I get that other people's problems are not our problems. We can't fix everything for everyone, and my pain is my issue. I deal with it. But I wish, sometimes, that people wouldn't assume I'm overreacting or have a low pain threshold. *No, Susan, I'm not that desperate for attention.*

I'm not faking it when I flinch or courting drama when I involuntarily convulse. And yes, your cousin's neighbour's sister's migraines sound awful too, and I'm glad giving up wheat helped.

I don't need sympathy. Okay, maybe a little. Coddling when you feel punk is nice. But understanding, that's the ice cream sundae with sprinkles on top. And if I never hear "again?" when I tell people I'm suffering through a flare, that'd be great. Chronic means chronic, in case you were curious. [15]

I get that my pain is a source of irritation and frustration for those around me. I'm sorry that people with chronic conditions are an inconvenience. Perhaps instead of getting irritated and impatient, the people who aren't afflicted could try empathy? Or even patience and a non-loaded silence?

I get that other people's problems can be difficult and inconvenient. How do you think the people who are actually suffering feel?

Be kind. You never know what someone is going through.

(March 3, 2020)

Nine: The Rise of the Eating Disorder Brain, Part 7,294.

The longer you've had your eating disorder, the harder it is to change the way you think. This isn't to say you can't recover. It just means the hard business of changing what you do is only the beginning. Fixing broken thinking patterns is where the real work lies. If you can't do that, you'll fall back into old behaviours. It's inevitable.

You don't notice how broken your thinking is when you're in the grips of the disease. I started noticing it more once I had solid time in with my behavioural changes. Suddenly, the "fat" thoughts, judgments, and directives were in the spotlight. Before, they were just background chatter, a soundtrack for the actions I took.

Noticing what the eating disorder is saying is a win, absolutely, but again only part of the process. The critical step lies in changing those thoughts. Challenging, countering, and rewriting them, so they're more suitable for the non-eating disordered person you're working on becoming.

I assume the final step is not having eating-disordered thoughts at all. I wish I had a timeline for when that might happen; unfortunately, rewiring neural pathways takes time.

It's odd how you have all the time in the world for the problem but can't bear to spend any time on the solution. I gave up decades to my eating disorder, yet I resent the time it's taking to get better. I want it fixed now. I want recovery to be faster.

I developed my eating disorder at age eleven; I added throwing up to my repertoire at age nineteen. Besides brief respites that occurred while I was in treatment, I continued vomiting multiple times a day nearly every day until five years ago. That's twenty-five years of purging. I didn't even abstain during pregnancy, much to my regret.

Five years ago, I went into treatment for what I hope will be the final time. It was an intervention-based decision and the fact that I was at "do or die" contributed to my willingness to accept help. I've spent my adult life determined to stop but unable to, even when I ended up in emergency rooms. I knew death was a possible consequence, but the threat didn't feel real. But things happened, and suddenly, it loomed close.

Get busy living or get busy dying. [16]

I only threw up twice while I was in treatment. That's two times in three and a half months, the best I'd managed since nineteen. More importantly, I was able to continue with some of the behavioural changes upon leaving. First, it was not throwing up for a few weeks at a time; then, it was abstaining for a few months. My latest run of vomit-free eating will reach eight months on Friday. I consider that to be a miracle.

The fallout from a prolonged eating disorder is perhaps something health practitioners don't emphasize enough in the early days. I might have fought harder if I knew the consequences of soft bones, organ problems, and essential toothlessness were pretty much guaranteed. I might have fought harder if they told me the eating disorder was making my depression worse. Or, maybe not. My desire wasn't qualified; it was thin at all costs. Still, late is better than never. At least that's what I tell myself.

The eating is reasonably stable, and the purging is pretty much under control, but I get disheartened at times because I still don't have my brain back. The sobriety that has been so hard-fought for is primarily of the body. I'd say my brain is about forty percent recovered. That is, I think I think like someone without an eating disorder forty percent of the time. The rest of the time is something else.

I still kind of believe I need to be thin to be acceptable. I still struggle to live in a body I vaguely dislike for being imperfect (though "vaguely dislike" is better than the extreme loathing I used to engage in). I still judge my worth by the amount of flesh I carry.

I still worry about my clothing size and my thigh gap and the diameter of my upper arms, and what kind of person I am if I'm physically imperfect. I also worry about what kind of person worries about such a shallow thing.

I also still restrict. Sometimes, I even pretend I think it's okay. Sometimes, I pretend the eating disorder voice isn't talking to me. Sometimes, I let it take me where it wants to go. Habit and the sixty percent, I suppose.

I wanted to lose some weight. I've maintained a recovery weight for a while; it's heavier than I'm comfortable with. I wanted to drop a few pounds. I went back and forth with myself for some time.

No, I shouldn't. Yes, I should. Other people lose ten pounds without getting sick. People recovering from eating disorders probably shouldn't diet. My legs are too soft and large. I'm an empirically small person. I'm not comfortable being this size. I should get comfortable, not lose weight. Back and forth, round and round.

I finally decided that trying to lose ten pounds would be okay as long as I improved my diet. Maybe more protein – something that's hard to re-introduce when you've had an eating disorder. More vegetables – I still tend to avoid sides. More fresh fruit.

It seemed like a good idea at the time. I should've been more suspicious of my eating disorder's silence. I should've talked about losing weight with my therapists – avoiding discussing the choices you're making with the experts trying to help you is a sign you should pay attention to.

At any rate, I went ahead, lost a little weight, cut back on my intake, started wearing baggy clothes, and watched my bones get more defined. I started revelling once again in the feelings of hunger that come from a reduced caloric intake.

Dangerous stuff. Slippery slopes.

I went back to using small bowls without even think about it. It's a common eating disorder thing. You use small dishes, small cutlery, small portions. It lets you believe the amounts you portion out are normal. You start thinking dinner in a half-cup bowl is a good thing.

Sneaky, sneaky, sneaky. Eating disorders and other addiction-style problems are sneaky. They don't want you to get unhooked. I get it: where would they go if you were better? They dig in. They mount covert campaigns.

I'm irritated with myself for succumbing. I'm irritated I went ahead with something I knew was a bad idea. However, I'm also chuffed I figured it out before things got out of hand. I recognized dangerous territory before things got dire. That's a win. Even so, the inside voice still thinks I should lose weight.

The "thoughts" part is the biggest challenge. It takes the most time. The defective thinking shows up everywhere, infects everything.

My current thinking is better than it has been for most of my adult life. It's not great thinking, it's not the thinking of someone who hasn't had an eating disorder, but I am improving. I still make odd bargains with food, I still eat in dysfunctional ways, and I still obsess over my imperfections.

There are wins. I eat three meals a day. I eat my snacks. I engage in moderate exercise only. I've avoided the temptation to eliminate whole categories of food for suspect motivations. I stay away from food fads. I try to say nice things to my hips and thighs, or at least not trash-talk them.

I'm working on liking myself and being comfortable in my skin.

But arguing with the eating disorder thoughts is the most important thing. I counter with logic. I counter with hate (that one might not be therapist-approved). I remind myself that fat isn't a feeling. I remember that most of the time, I don't want to end up dead.

I get impatient but rewiring the brain takes as long as it takes. One day, I'll be able to exercise for twenty minutes and enjoy the experience.

I won't argue with myself about doing ten minutes more because my body needs serious work.

I won't consider making the proposed extra ten an extra twenty because, thighs.

I won't think about how forty minutes every day for a week would mean I could lose five pounds by Sunday, and wouldn't that be great?

Eventually, my brain will get there. Eventually, I won't have to reformat my thoughts. Eventually, I'll order the first food that appeals on the menu without checking out the salads. Until then, you just keep doing the work. You argue with your eating disorder voice. You remind yourself *ad nauseum* the eating disorder is a liar. You ignore the little voices that tell you it's too hard and taking too long. You get ready for battle 7,295 because, why not?

What else am I going to do with my time but work on recovery? It's a reasonable pursuit to engage in (some of the time: don't make it your life). Besides, I know how re-engaging with my eating disorder ends.

(January 14, 2020)

Ten: My Eating Disorder.

You got up this morning, stretched, and staggered into the kitchen. Depending on your preference, you waited impatiently for coffee or tea before getting started on your morning routine.

You showered, got dressed, and got ready to face the day, at work or at home. Maybe breakfast, maybe not.

Lunchtime rolled around, and you were hungry, so you grabbed some food. Perhaps you got a meal from a fast-food restaurant; maybe you made yourself a sandwich. Mid-afternoon, you had some chips and a pop. You were going to make something for dinner, but friends called, so you headed out to the pub for some appetizers and dinner and maybe even a beer.

Once back home after an enjoyable evening, you did a few chores, watched some tv, grabbed another snack, and eventually headed off to bed. As you were brushing your teeth, you realized you didn't get in any exercise but shrugged, figuring you'd get to it tomorrow.

You didn't count calories today: you didn't give much thought to what you ate at all. You didn't call yourself foul names for being lazy and skipping a workout, you didn't drop to the bathroom floor to do pushups, and it never once occurred to you to throw up your dinner.

You fell asleep without checking for protruding bones.

*

I haven't had a day like that since I was eleven-years-old: that's a long time to go without touching normal.

I remember the moment my eating disorder took over. I was an insecure and self-conscious young girl. I wanted to fit in, not be the oddity I perceived myself as being. I desperately needed approval; I needed people to tell me I was okay because I felt anything but. I've felt less than, inadequate, inferior, and not enough my whole life. I think it's baked into my bones.

I found out my problems existed because I was fat near the end of grade five, though I'd already started to suspect. I was sitting in the school field with two friends, let's call them Sherri and Terri. [17] I wanted to be best friends with Sherri more than anything; I wanted to be her first choice. I needed it. Being picked first would mean I wasn't the fundamental failure I suspected. I would belong. I would be okay.

Our conversation before and after the defining moment is lost to time, but the moment itself remains clear decades on. Sherri told me, apropos of nothing while we were all sitting in the field after school, that Terri was her best friend and I was only second-best. I can still feel the tight chest of a mortal emotional wound. I looked down at my lap as I sat there trying to disappear, trying to make the pain go away and thought to myself, *"Your legs are fat."* I knew then that my thighs were the source of my problem. If they were thinner, if I were thinner, I would've been the best friend. Then I wouldn't feel rejected, wouldn't feel pain. If I were thinner, things would be right.

I wish I'd said, "To hell with you" and stomped off, but bravery in the face of anticipated rejection is a tricky thing, and I didn't know I was enough, as is.

*

I've met people who, after learning about my eating disorder, are eager to share their own trip down that dark path. That they travelled only inches doesn't distract from their self-bestowed expertise.

They talk about how they were bulimic one summer at camp when they decided as a group to throw up dinner for the week. They were cured once they returned home. They talk about how they used to be anorexic because they ate only fruit and lost 15 pounds, but they stopped, and they've been fine ever since.

Many people lay claim to a brief eating disorder in their attempts to commiserate. Implicit in their stories is the accusatory "why": why can't I stop when they did it so easily? I would have if I could. Having every moment be an exercise in self-hatred and negative judgment is problematic. Unfortunately, I'd travelled rather more than inches before I started trying to change course.

I try to be understanding but conversations like the above end up making me angry. We're not the same. Riding a horse on a trail ride on the weekend doesn't make me a cowboy, and a few months of aberrant eating doesn't mean you have an eating disorder. Count yourself lucky you quit before it took.

Until last week, I was eight-months sober in my eating-disorder behaviour. Mostly. I'm eating in a fairly non-eating disordered way with three meals and a couple of snacks. There's also been no excessive exercising and no vomiting. The "minimal" for chemical purging is why I call it "mostly sober," but my intestines are not yet functioning properly. This is the longest I've been abstinent from eating disorder behaviours since I was nineteen.

Eating disorders are hell. They have the highest mortality rate of any mental illness. (It makes me a little proud to state that: that's probably sad. It's like being proud that my chronic pain, neuralgia, is one of the worst. Negative attention is not good attention!) I'm still trying to figure out how to describe its hellish and soul-destroying nature without being revoltingly graphic.

Sharing has consequences beyond weirdly-competitive commiseration. Eating disorders are like fight club: the first rule is we don't talk about fight club. It strikes back if you share. The blowback from opening up can be challenging and dangerous: eating disorder practices, while repulsive, strange, and obscene to those on the outside, are dire and deadly for those of us living here.

Sometimes, I try to turn my experiences into funny anecdotes I can share. *"Did I tell you about turning orange? Apparently, eating only carrots for a month is a bad idea: I developed vitamin A toxicity."* Hilarious.

Or the story about the first time I took an emetic. I misjudged the amount of time it would take to start working and ended up vomiting on myself while driving on the freeway. Nothing says "funny" like a steering wheel and lap covered in puke. What I remember most is my weeping.

An eating disorder isn't a game. It's starving yourself until you can't sleep, think, or do anything but wait for the next small food allotment. It's driving from fast food restaurant to fast food restaurant while shoving food down your throat so fast it has no taste, and then vomiting in an alley until the blood vessels in your eyes burst. It's learning to shop at different stores, so no one is aware of your reality. It's lying to cashiers about this or that upcoming party so they don't question the cakes and ice cream. It's exercising for four hours straight and hating the flesh on your bones. It's thousands and thousands of dollars spent on food you throw up, exercise equipment you abuse, and medications that help you purge.

It's eating for an hour and throwing up for an hour, over and over for days on end until you pass out. It's vomiting until blood drips from your lacerated esophagus and seeps from the infected sores on your hands, caused by your teeth as you force your fingers down your throat. It's shoplifting laxatives, water pills, emetics, and mouthwash because your habit is expensive and you've run out of money, but you need. It's ulcers in your stomach, a devastated bone density, and teeth that rot and fall out. It's knowing you're killing yourself and being desperate to stop but continuing the behaviour anyhow. It's starving yourself for a month and then binging for three days straight. It's suicidal thoughts and attempts. It's praying for death because you can't live in the hell your life has become.

It isn't a transitory thing you try on. It isn't a crash diet. It isn't a game or a joke. It's doctors who don't understand you, nurses who deride you, emergency room personnel who judge you, and ambulance drivers who think you're wasting their time. It's a family you're devastating and friends who beg you to get help because you're killing yourself slowly. It's wanting help but being too afraid to accept it because "help" means "fat," and that would leave you a failure.

It's hell.

I'm back to being sober in my eating after falling off the wagon the last week. Getting closer to sober with the thinking is more complex, especially since I was nowhere close yet. I'm action, not thought. I still struggle with my body. I struggle to believe I have value beyond the skeletal. I struggle to believe people care about me; that they like me even if I'm not perfect. I struggle with learning to be me. I want to say "to hell with you" to the people out there that judge, criticize, and detract, and I want to mean it.

But for now, I'll take today and sober eating and consider myself blessed.

(December 3, 2015, September 14, 2019)

Eleven: Not About the Body.

An eating disorder isn't really about the body. The problem originates elsewhere. It's history, nature, both, and neither. That's what makes treatment challenging. Everyone comes from a different place. There's no eating disorder penicillin.

For me, anxiety is a large piece of the puzzle. The historical happenings are significant, but my anxious nature is why my compensatory behaviours went the way they did. Anxiety feels unbearable: the relief the eating disorder promised was too good to pass up.

Suddenly, the uncomfortable feelings had a focus – my physical imperfections. By focusing on my body and engaging in distracting behaviours designed to perfect it, I could, at last, subdue the feelings that made me want to crawl out of my skin.

But because the real problems have nothing to do with the body, working on the body doesn't provide a fix. It does, however, distract for periods of time. And since that feels like relief, we re-commit to our actions, creating a vicious cycle of maladaptive coping mechanism, anxiety, and repeat.

An eating disorder will never make things better. It only ever makes things worse. Once you're in it, however, escape is difficult. An added problem is desire: you get a little Stockholm Syndrome with it. We might say we want to get better, but truthfully, most of the time, we want the crutch behaviour more. We don't want to feel the uncomfortable feelings to come back. Blood in the throat is easier.

Compounding the escape problem is the reality that abstinence is not an option. We have to eat to survive. People with eating disorders are forever tied to their drug of choice.

Nature or nurture: who's to blame for all of this? Anxiety is my nature, but treatment and experiences are part of the puzzle as well. I could hop on the "blame the parents" bandwagon, but not much was their fault. The same nature that made me anxious also blocked me from approaching them for help: I'm the fixer and caretaker. That I've always felt fundamentally flawed made things harder. I'll ask for help when I'm better.

I tried hard to get perfect. I tried for a long time, but I kept failing. I'd do all the things the eating disorder suggested, but I was still wrong. I was still imperfect. I should've concluded the plan was flawed. Unfortunately, the eating disorder doesn't let you go there. The problem is always and ever you.

Eating disorders are also a growth proposition. They expand and become about more than food and the body. Soon, everything needs to be perfect. It's hard to resist the lures the defective thoughts dangle, always promising that this time, with this behaviour, it'll work.

The eating disorder is such a liar.

You can't fix yourself this way. You don't know that, though. In the early days, you think you've found the magic secret, the trick that will make everything okay. Even if you think about it being an eating disorder, you don't worry. You're in control. You don't notice when things start to go bad because the eating disorder breaks the mind-body connection. We're meant to be a single entity. The eating disorder breaks us into pieces, and suddenly, the mind and body are at war. Wars are not about communication.

Re-establishing the mind-body connection is challenging. It's been five years since I started working seriously on recovery, and my body still feels like the enemy too much of the time. It's hard to let that go, surprisingly hard to silence a voice that only has negative and hurtful things to say.

An acquaintance once told me that emotional healing takes about half the time you had invested in the problematic situation. I was married for seven years and felt entirely over it a little past the "three-years since separation" mark. A sobering thought when I look at my numbers: I have almost forty years of an eating disorder under my belt.

Freedom sixty-five. Something to celebrate.

(July 27, 2020)

Twelve: Thoughts About Your Relationship with Yourself.

I don't spend much time thinking about the quality of the relationship I have with myself. I'm just there.

I don't think I'm uncommon. We're not taught to spend time on the relationship we have with ourselves, to analyze and improve it. Which is strange when you consider its duration.

Too many of us are not our own best friends. We treat ourselves poorly at worst and as an afterthought at best. We need to do better. We will never have another relationship that is as close or intimate. And, a better relationship with yourself improves your relationship with other people. Seeking better is a win-win.

Not reflecting on my relationship with myself seems odd when you consider how I spend my days. I learn about self-love and self-care and depression and mental health and philosophy and eating disorders. I implement procedural changes but fail to spend an equal amount of time thinking about the way I think and changing my fundamental beliefs. If you don't dig out the root, it'll keep sending up shoots.

I take my relationship with myself for granted. Sometimes we do okay. There are times when I don't think nasty thoughts or hurt myself, when I treat myself well.

Then there are the other days, days when the relationship becomes abusive.

I try to mitigate the abuse when I become aware but again, primarily through behavioural changes. I haven't worked hard enough on the nature of the relationship itself. It doesn't feel urgent. I don't feel the same kind of pressure with my relationship with myself that I do with others. I don't care about taking care. After all, it's not like I can leave myself when things go badly. Where would I go?

I choose to spend time on the relationships I have with other people. It's a conscious effort. I work hard on being a good friend. I maintain contact, I listen, I remember the important stuff, and I'm there if things get rough. [18] I try to treat them well. I don't expect relationships to be effort-free.

Except for the one I have with myself.

I should attend to it more. It's important. I read a comment recently that summed things up nicely:

"no one is going to be with me forever other than me (body, mind, soul). That is a fact. So, I better take better care of myself. This is not selfish as long as [I] don't take care of [myself] at the expense of others." -Betal Erbasi

My problem is with the architecture. I built a house with damaged material. Instead of committing myself to the complicated structural repairs, I use behavioural changes to shore up the cracks. It's like putting out a bucket for a leak. It's a temporary fix, and the underlying problem remains. As long as it does, the patch won't hold.

I think some part of me hoped the relationship would change naturally, that I'd automatically become more of a friend to myself as I work on my neuroses. I think part of me hoped my thinking would evolve and improve without additional work. That I would be able to write over the bad code without looking at it and making deep edits. It doesn't work that way. If I don't chase the thoughts back to their point of origin and making repairs there, too, the problems will continue to recur.

The work has been partially effective: my external behaviours are improving. But they'll feel awkwardly unnatural until I change the underneath. I just don't like to go there. It's dark and uncomfortable and sad.

It'll be hard, and I like easy.

It's also necessary.

Danger, Will Robinson. Hard work and difficult times lie ahead. It will probably be worth it, at least when I come out on the other side. Because when you dislike yourself, when you're fundamentally dissatisfied with who you are as a human being, your ability to enjoy your life is diminished. And time's passing.

How to improve your relationship with yourself. [19]

1. Value yourself. Embrace your strengths and weaknesses. Own who you are and learn to accept it. Better, learn to like it. Let go of dual standards: the ones you apply to yourself versus those you apply to others.

2. Embrace your strengths and weaknesses. Let go of the need for perfection: do things your way and congratulate yourself on being authentic. Get comfortable with feeling uncomfortable. Get comfortable with things being messy. Life isn't a clean and tidy business. Be real with yourself. Listen to your circle. Hear the things they tell you about yourself: stop self-deprecating and practicing false modesty. It's okay to be awesome.

3. *Take care of your own needs.* You can't address things like love, belonging, and self-esteem if your basic needs for physical and psychological safety aren't being met. * Make yourself healthy and safe first before moving on to more complex problems.

4. *Make time for happiness.* Things that bring you joy and contentment are good things: prioritize them. Would you want a friendship with someone who always put you last and didn't care about what you like or makes you happy?

5. *Make time for yourself.* You can't be a friend to someone who's never there. How can you hope to understand and appreciate yourself if you never spend time with yourself, getting to know you? Get to know yourself intimately, all the bits and pieces. Journaling and meditation help with this. The latter is particularly helpful in developing an open-minded and compassionate outlook, which is a good quality for a friend to have.

6. *Boundaries.* Yes, it always comes back to them. You can develop a better relationship with yourself if you respect yourself. Having and enforcing boundaries is a big part of that.

7. *Accept failure.* Failure isn't the end of the world, and it doesn't say anything about your worth as a person. It's okay to fail. It's also inevitable, so accept that reality. You're not now, nor have you been, nor will you be perfect.

8. *Volunteer*. It comes up often as a way to make ourselves feel good as human beings. We're better friends when we're altruistic. It's a winning choice.

* [Maslow's *Hierarchy of Needs*]

(January 28, 2020)

Appendix: What doesn't kill you, blah, blah, blah.

People like to say, *"what doesn't kill you makes you stronger."* If that were true, I'd be Atlas by now.

I'm back from my week-long, run-away-from-home vacation to Mexico. I lasted four days, and I'm struggling with feeling like a failure. It's hard to believe I made the best decision when I called my parents in tears and asked them to book me a flight home: I was too distressed to do it myself, my iPhone interface too tricky for my state of mind.

I've been sliding back into depression and struggling with my eating disorder for some time now. I'd hoped the time away in the sun, relaxing and drinking on a beach would help. Things didn't play out according to plan.

I'd planned on a week of calm. I'd planned to relax, participate, and interact. I'd planned on being "not me." It didn't work out.

Alone was fine until I passed through airport security, and my brain started attacking. I worked hard on counteracting it. I talked to people at the airport and on the plane. I interacted at the beach and the pool. I went to the shows and sat at the bar. I pretended, over and over, that I felt okay.

I was a bit lonely, the loneliness of not being in a relationship when everyone around you seems to be. You wonder what's wrong with you, why you can't find a person to walk through life with. My fear of men probably has something to do with it, though my eating disorder likes to blame it on the size of my thighs. If my legs were perfect, I'd have a perfect partner.

I love the ocean. I love the sun and the waves and the smells and the sounds. Until my brain tells me to swim out and never stop. That's what it is to have suicidal ideation. Like when you're strolling along the road, and you hear a car behind you, and your brain tells you to step left.

I was sitting on my balcony, watching the sun and the waves, but the voice urging me to jump got so distracting, I sat on the ground and crawled back inside. I started crying when I got there because what the fuck is wrong with me? Why can't I just vacation in Mexico?

I did all the things I "should." I tried not to attend to my thoughts. I tried countering them with positives. I practiced distraction and stayed busy. I tried not worrying about my smoking and drinking and eating: I tried to be easy on myself instead.

It helped for moments at a time, but the thoughts kept coming back, louder and more insistent. It's a strange thing to be afraid of yourself. It's odd to feel unsafe when help is so far away. "Home" was the only thing I could focus on amidst the noise of my thoughts. I wanted my safe space, with my safe things, and my safe routine.

Perhaps solo travel is not for me? Maybe a friend could've helped me through, though I struggle to share: I don't want to be the downer. But I wasn't with anyone, I was on my own, and I was afraid. Impulse can be a killer.

And so, I left, three days earlier than planned. I'm working hard on not calling myself a failure all hours of the day. My eating disorder is thrilled; she likes it when I screw up. She's been busy since I returned, drawing up plans for a new diet and exercise program: things would've been perfect with ten pounds less.

I'm home. I'm safe. I'm trying to remember I accomplished things. Like travelling alone and not ending up dead.

Now that I'm home and the panic is fading, I'm remembering. Not everything was a failure.

I wasn't universally reviled and shunned, for instance. I was worried about that.

The people I met liked me well enough to talk to me and spend time with me. That was a shock that helped alleviate my fear that I'm only ever accepted because of the company I keep: when you're by yourself, that doesn't fly.

I'm also still competent. I can navigate through life. I worried about that; about the effect my prolonged disability time-off has had. But I can still function in the "real" world.

The critical thing to remember is that although things didn't go to plan, there were positives to be had. One other thing, however, became very clear.

I suffer from mental illness.

I've talked about it, lived it, been treated for it, and seen counsellors and doctors. It's caused problems in my personal and professional life. It shows up everywhere. And even with all that, a small part of me wants to believe the problem was I'm weak and pathetic and lazy.

But I was lying in bed, watching *Baywatch* in Spanish after not jumping off the balcony, having set the wheels in motion for my return when I realized the truth of my reality. Not everyone is like this. This is what it means to have mental illness. Some things are harder for me. Sometimes, I need help.

It's not my fault, and it doesn't have to define me any more than my mother's diabetes has to define her. But I have to take care of it, pay attention to the symptoms, and address problems quickly to avoid things escalating.

If that means leaving vacation early to stay safe, that's okay.

I just need to remember that in the moment.

(April 5, 2019)

Help and Support.

This is by no means a comprehensive list, and I make no claims about the quality of help they provide. The truth is, you'll encounter hits and misses before you find the program or person that clicks. I tried to provide contacts for the major geographic areas. If I missed yours, I'm sorry.

Remember, too, that recovery is a verb. I didn't do the work for a long time. I don't get those years back, and that's a shame and a source of regret. I wish you otherwise.

1. Canada:

NEDIC (National Eating Disorder Information Centre)

Toll-Free: 1-866-NEDIC-20

(Toronto: 416-340-4156)

email: nedic@uhn.ca,

chat: https://nedic.ca/

2. USA:

NEDA (National Eating Disorders Association)

Toll-Free Phone Number: 1-800-931-2237

Monday to Thursday 11:00 a.m. to 9:00 p.m. ET and Friday 11:00 a.m. to 5:00 p.m. ET.

For crisis support, text 'NEDA' to 741741

(Helpline text pilot hours are Monday-Thursday, 3:00 p.m. to 6:00 p.m. ET.
Helpline chat hours are Monday-Thursday 9:00 a.m. to 9:00 p.m. ET and
Friday 9:00 a.m. to 5:00 p.m. ET.)

3. Mexico:

Eating Disorder Referral (www.edreferral.com/Mexico)

Mexican Association for the Treatment of Eating Disorders,
amta@campus.iztacala.unam.mx

4. United Kingdom:

Beat Eating Disorders

UK Helpline: 0808 801 0677 , Student-line: 0808 801 0811 , Youth-line: 0808
801 0711

Helplines are open 365 days a year from 9:00 a.m. to 9:00 p.m. during the week
and 4:00 p.m. to 8:00 p.m. on weekends and bank holidays. Sometimes, our
lines are busy. If you can't get through immediately, please do try again or try
our one-to-one webchat.

If you need urgent help for yourself or someone else outside of our Helpline
opening hours, if you or someone else is in immediate danger, please
contact 999 or the Samaritans on 116 123.

5. Republic of Ireland:

The College of Irish Psychiatry

Andrea Ryder, andrea@irishpsychiatry.ie 01 634 4774, Karen McCourt, kmccourt@irishpsychiatry.ie 01 634 4374, Ian Rice, irice@irishpsychiatry.ie 01 634 4374

6. European Union:

Eating Disorders Treatment in EU and USA by Jelena Balabanić Mavrović.

https://www.centarbea.hr/sites/default/files/ED%20treatment%20EU%20%26%20USA_2018_0.pdf

7. Asia, Southeast Asia,

Thailand: NCS Counselling, (66) 02 114 7556, https://ncsbkk.com/ncs/

Singapore: Singapore General Hospital, (65) 6222 3322, https://www.sgh.com.sg/

Australia/New Zealand: ANZAED, Australia: (+61) 491 134 289, New Zealand: (+64) 9 887 0552, https://www.anzaed.org.au/

8. South America.

ALUBA (Asociacion de Lucha contra la Bulimia y la Anorexia) is also on Twitter, Facebook, and Instagram. https://aluba.org.ar/

About the Author.

Kathleen (for the "K") Michelle Pahl uses her middle name. She gets annoyed when people get weird about it, which happens more often than you'd think. It's sexist: no one bats an eye at C. Montgomery Burns' choice.

She's also uncertain about the kind of information required for the "about the author" page, notwithstanding the plethora of examples available. Should she mention her doll collection? Should she mention she rarely reads much about the authors (actors, musicians) she enjoys? Should she point out that she tends to drift into third-person while writing, an annoying habit that leads to much revision?

I don't stalk people whose work I stan because I'm interested in what they produce, not in their lives' minutiae (though I like to make sure they aren't evil). Nevertheless, a few details, like age, location, and appearance, are satisfying to know.

The nitty-gritty, then. I'm Canadian, and I live in British Columbia, as I have for most of my fifty-one years. I have a university degree in Political Science, a field I chose because it had the least graduation requirements. I wanted a Renaissance education, but that wasn't an option. I gave some thought to law, but I'm unsuited: the television-based raging in the courtroom that appeals isn't a thing that's allowed.

I've struggled to hold down jobs for any length of time: health issues, some physical but most mental, have interfered. Nevertheless, I try. I think. Maybe. I've at least persisted. Mostly and kind of.

I also spend time being a mediocre sister, weak aunt, and less-than-ideal daughter. The standards set by sit-coms are hard to meet.

I have anxiety, depression, and PTSD, in addition to my eating disorder. I like to describe myself as neurotic. It means "to have neuroses," but I enjoy the "you're crazy" subtext.

I'm working on my recovery. It's ongoing, and it takes time. The "time" thing annoys me: I was hoping for instant recovery, decades of illness notwithstanding.

In the early days, especially, I wanted to give up. To quit quitting. There are a million reasons not to recover. You can always come up with excuses for staying sick.

One of the biggies is the belief that it's different for you. Sure, other people have eating disorders, but not like you. This is the enormous ED lie we choose to believe. We aren't different. We aren't special. We're one of many.

Millions of people have eating disorders. They starve, vomit, chew and spit, obsess over pure foods, purge, hate themselves, torture themselves, over-exercise, and die from their eating disorder. There's no unique there. There's only waste.

There's no upside to an eating disorder. The best time to stop was yesterday. The second-best time is now. [20]

Connect with the author.

Thank you for reading. I appreciate your interest and support more than I can say. If you enjoyed the book or found it helpful in any way, please leave a review. If you'd like to keep in touch, don't hesitate to connect with me on social media. [21]

Facebook: https://www.facebook.com/faminetofeasting

Blog: http://fromfaminetofeast-eatingdisordersandrecovery.com

Smashwords: https://www.smashwords.com/profile/view/empahla

Pinterest: https://pin.it/7vWqeDS

Twitter: https://twitter.com/pahl_brighteyes

Endnotes

---

[1] Effusive and over-the-top?

[2] Cedars at Cobble Hill Addiction Rehabilitation Centre
3741 Holland Ave, Cobble Hill, BC V0R 1L0
1-866-716-2006
https://cedarscobblehill.com/.

[3] I struggle with the effects of Post-Traumatic Stress Disorder. Mood volatility and difficulty dealing with frustrations are a part of that. I took a medication that helped for nearly three years, but the side-effects ultimately proved unbearable. I'm currently trying to live without pharmacological help for my PTSD.

[4] There are thirteen chapters in my "top twelve" book, not including sneaky, non-blog additions. I blame WikiHow: the book's structure and the additional sections are recommended in the "How to Publish on Kindle" post.
https://www.wikihow.com/Publish-on-Kindle

[5] I named my blog "From Famine to Feast" to illustrate the direction recovery takes (ideally) while still giving a nod to my eating disorder.
http://fromfaminetofeast-eatingdisordersandrecovery.com

[6] I'm fairly fond of alliteration.

[7] "Music hath charms to soothe a savage breast." William Congreve. We'll pretend my near-obsessive need for balance and straight lines is an "everyone" thing.

[8] It's not like I planned on only using exotics. Am I the only one who hates the binary choice between Arial and Times New Roman?

[9] I'm not the first and I won't be the last.

[10] Reviewing an old post is an interesting experience. Some of the behaviours have been abandoned. Some are still a problem. Perhaps they're hardwired, part of my operating system that requires a permanent workaround? I've more work to do, even three years on. I wish I'd considered the consequences carefully when I was younger, when I stepped into my eating disorder. I like to think I'd have chosen better if I'd thought on it. But, probably not. I started at eleven. Not an age known for forward-thinking.

[11] I say, "I love you, Michelle." This works for me since "Michelle" is my name. Obviously, you have a name of your own. Use that one. Unless your name is Michelle, too. In which case, feel free to copy the phrase I use.

[12] "Nevertheless, she persisted" became the rallying cry around Senator Warren (USA) in 2018 in the face of rank sexism. https://www.washingtonpost.com/news/the-fix/wp/2017/02/08/nevertheless-she-persisted-becomes-new-battle-cry-after-mcconnell-silences-elizabeth-warren/

[13] The sentence ends with a preposition. Some people consider this a writing sin, on par with excessive descriptors. I'm not sure why we have adverbs and adjectives if they're not to be used. Regarding prepositions, I remember an anecdote attributed to the complicated Sir Winston Churchill, his response when criticized for the same infraction: *this is the type of errant pedantry up with which I will not put.* I will direct Grammarly accordingly.

[14] As it turns out, COVID19 happened. At least I wasn't stuck with a two-week quarantine.

[15] If you were looking for a definition that wasn't snide and testy, chronic means, "persisting for a long time or constantly recurring." Chronic pain is the Terminator of pain. It'll be back.

[16] I'm paraphrasing from *The Shawshank Redemption (film, 1994)*. "I guess it comes down to a simple choice really. Get busy living or get busy dying." I adore that sentence by Andy Dufresne (used later by Red Redding). It's like Frank's Red-Hot Sauce. I put that shit on everything. I should live it more. https://www.imdb.com/title/tt0111161/

---

[17] I stole the names from the evil-ish twins on *The Simpsons,* Sherri and Terri Mackleberry. Forty years on and I still feel salty about the whole thing. I need to let it go.

[18] I'm amazing. Practically perfect. Definitely hyperbolic. Sigh. I'm a good friend some of the time. I'm bad at it some of the time, too. The same is true for my other roles: sister, daughter, and mom. I do try. But I'm not the amazingly special snowflake my wounded sense of pride likes to imagine. I'm no Mary Poppins, practically perfect in every way.

[19] My resources: https://www.bustle.com/p/7-unexpected-but-amazingly-effective-ways-to-improve-your-relationship-with-yourself-7925162, https://psychcentral.com/blog/6-ways-you-can-have-a-healthy-relationship-with-yourself/, https://www.simplypsychology.org/maslow.html

[20] My twist on a popular Chinese proverb: "The best time to plant a tree was 20 years ago. The second-best time is now." If you want success in the future, act.

[21] I talk about politics and politicians a lot. At least on Twitter. I also skew to the left. The blog is mostly politics free, though I do believe that basically, politics is life.